Solving for X

Solving for X

Robert B. Shaw

OHIO UNIVERSITY PRESS

ATHENS

Ohio University Press, Athens, Ohio 45701

© 2002 by Robert B. Shaw

Printed in the United States of America

Ohio University Press books are printed on acid-free paper ⊗ ™

10 09 08 07 06 05 04 03 02   5 4 3 2 1

Library of Congress Cataloging-in-Publication Data
Shaw, Robert Burns, 1947–
    Solving for x : poems / Robert B. Shaw.
        p. cm.
    ISBN 0-8214-1471-2 (alk. paper) — ISBN 0-8214-1472-0 (pbk. : alk. paper)
        I. Title.

PS3569.H3845 S65 2002
811'.54—dc21

                                        2002027092

Acknowledgments

Acknowledgment is made to the editors of the following publications in which several of the poems in this book first appeared: *The Dark Horse, Janus, The Nation, The New Criterion, The Sewanee Review, Shenandoah, Southwest Review,* and *The Yale Review.* "A Paper Cut," "Remainders," "Called Back," "Solving for X," "QWERTY," "Letter of Recommendation," "Making Do," "Up and Away," "Other Eyes," "Waste," "Waiting Room," and "Out of Character" first appeared in *Poetry.* "Wishing Well" is reprinted from volume 3, number 1 of *Literary Imagination: The Review of the Association of Literary Scholars and Critics,* © 2001. Used by permission of the ALSC. "Drowned Towns" and "The Devil's Garden" appeared in a chapbook co-authored with Edgar Bowers and William Conelly: *Drowned Towns and Other Poems of Place* (Hatfield, Mass.: The Van Zora Press, 2000). "Shoptalk: Ten Epigrams" appeared in the chapbook anthology *Profile Full Face* (Hatfield, Mass.: The Van Zora Press, 2001).

Many of the facts in "Drowned Towns" are drawn from two books by J. R. Greene: *The Creation of Quabbin Reservoir* and *The Day Four Quabbin Towns Died,* both published by The Transcript Press, Athol, Massachusetts. Other material was derived from informational booklets available at the Quabbin Visitors' Center.

For Timothy Steele

Increasing with the years but still bicoastal,
our friendship has perforce been mostly postal.
Accept this parcel, bearing scraps of gray
New England weather to you in L.A.,
as well as thanks for each new poem or letter
I welcome as a nudge to make mine better.

Contents

Solving for X

The Future Perfect

It will be recognizable: your neighborhood,
with of course some of the bigger trees
gone for pulp and the more upscale houses
sporting new riot-proof fencing which
they seem hardly to need in this calm sector
whose lawns look even more vacuumed than they used to.
Only a soft whirr of electric automobiles
ruffles unburdened air. Your own house looks
about the same, except for the solar panels.
Inside, the latest occupants sit facing
the wall-size liquid crystal flat TV screen
they haggle and commune with, ordering beach towels
or stockings, or instructing their stockbrokers,
while in the kitchen dinner cooks itself.
Why marvel over windows that flip at a touch
from clear to opaque, or carpets that a lifetime
of scuffs will never stain? This all was destined,
down to the newest model ultrasound toothbrush.
Only the stubborn, ordinary ratio
of sadness to happiness seems immune to progress,
and it will take more time than even you
have at your disposal to find out why.
The same and not the same, this venue fascinates,
spiriting you through closed familiar doors
on random unremarkable evenings when
you will have been gone
for how long? — Just a bit longer than your successors

have had to make these premises their own.
However much their climate-controlled rooms
glow vibrant with halogen, they will not see you.
But they may wonder why, for no clear reason,
they find their thoughts so often drawn to the past.

Back Again

The wormy apple tree
we chainsawed to a stump
is not content to be
a barren amputee.
It has produced a clump
of rank and spindly shoots,
a thicket still unthinned,
each one a witch's wand,
suggesting that the roots
regard our surgery
as one more hostile thing
to overcome in spring,
like parried blades of wind—
mischief to live beyond.

A Bowl of Stone Fruit

Never forget the child's face, nonplused
on touching first an apple, then a pear,
then a banana, his bewildered stare
becoming peevish as his buoyant trust

in the appearances that grown-ups prize
founders. Items for which his taste buds lusted
are for display, and regularly dusted.
Try to explain how people feast their eyes

on such a centerpiece, how they are able
to cherish a quartz peach, whose blushing skin
is bonded pigment, stone bearing within
no stone a tree would spring from. Now the table

stands taller than his head; but watch him grow,
to grow unflustered by the cold and hard
baubles adult taste holds in fond regard.
Never forget his face, first made to know.

Airs and Graces

All this was years ago—back in the days
of afternoon visits between ladies
with children brought along, resigned to boredom.
Her mother always stayed for a second cup;
her mother's aunt, happy to be a hostess,
kept pressing macaroons on her niece
and grand-niece (something neither of them favored).
It always seemed to be raining when they went there
and there was no dog or cat to play with.
When the women were tired of glancing sideways
to see her fidgeting or shedding crumbs,
they'd send her to the spare room to explore
the Dress-Up Box. This could be interesting
if she was in the mood for vintage glamour.

The Box was really a modest-sized tin trunk,
lined with flowered wallpaper and filled
with bits of swank from several decades back.
There were a few dresses, much too large,
trimmed with velvet and imbued with camphor.
It was the accessories she was drawn to.
There was a pair of white gloves that on her
were almost elbow-length. The missing buttons
forced her to bunch them at her wrists, so that
she looked like a Walt Disney character.
There were various paper-and-bamboo fans
with orchids and pagodas painted on them.
She fanned her face with these and made her bangs flap.

What else? A pin made of a real seashell,
a set of tortoise-shell combs, a rhinestone bracelet.
More intriguing: an oblong of black lace,
a shawl or a mantilla, that she always
spread out before her eyes while she decided
just how to drape it. Looking through its fine,
close-knotted mesh gave her a view like one
she could have got through a sooty window screen.
Two or three hats with feathers of no color
she'd ever seen on a bird sat carefully nested.

Best of all, always to be admired,
there was a brown, weaselly-looking fur piece,
that ringed her neck and dangled down her front,
the eyes studding its narrow nut of a head
inky black and hard as rock, the nose
rubbery-feeling like an old eraser.
A little chain could cinch the snout and tail
together, but the fixed jaws wouldn't bite.

There, in the little stuffy almost-attic,
trying these in their different combinations
before a mirror, practicing to be old
and regal, she could lose track of the time.
She grew oblivious to the parlor voices
talking about people she'd never known.
Finally, when her appearance satisfied her,
she paced grandly down, the funeral veil
swathing her hair, the spineless animal
bobbling to her waist. Her mother gasped
and clapped her hands. Her great-aunt smiled briefly,

then looked into her teacup. Years would pass
before the festooned girl would realize what
her hostess must have seen: her bygone self
and her dead sisters, flaunting these fine items
when they were new, and later not so new.

The First Mosquito

Still warm, still damp. Twilight.
Emboldened to impinge,
the whining parasite
administers a twinge,

a punctual siphoning
announcing summer's prime.
Too small to call a sting,
the lump she left this time

vouches for blood she needed
to spawn what will in turn
go forth to do as she did.
We might as well adjourn—

indoors. With skin awoken
to June so pointedly,
we'll settle for one token
of such phlebotomy.

A Field of Goldenrod

Midas, your fabled gleaming touch
would be hard put to burnish much
that ocher crop across the road—
like some erupting mother lode,
proliferating uncontrolled
back to the treeline, solid gold.
In truth, I doubt you could enhance
one August field's extravagance
by any glitter you could lend.
This is the wealth of summer's end;
an alchemy within the weed
will flaunt itself to scatter seed,
and summer, in a mood to splurge,
will outdo any thaumaturge.

Anthology Piece

Why, I sometimes wonder, out of all
the spirited conceptions of my Maker,
am I the chosen one? Reprinted ceaselessly,
misprinted sometimes (I have had death appear
in place of dearth, and yes, there is a difference),
memorized by the multitude—why me?
Something in my unmistakable rhythm
seems to have taken readers by the ear;
or could it be my undemanding scenery,
dusty road pointing ahead to sunset?
Woven snugly together with accustomed
sentiments toward all that's transitory . . .
What could be simpler? By this time I might
be sick of it myself, were I not bound
to bless my access to eternity.
As for the man who set my sky ablaze,
he grew to loathe my popular appeal,
but of course wasn't able to disown me.
Once I was plumper: seven lines, some good,
didn't survive the last slash of his pen.
(You'd never know: he didn't save the drafts.)
Now I am all that keeps his name alive,
pressed by hundreds of pages front and back.
Saffron pyres flicker on my horizon.
He'd have pissed on the embers if he could.

The End of the Sonnet

A word was missing from his fourteenth line.
He mused on how much easier it would be
if one could still wedge an apostrophe
in "over," or if cattle still were kine,
when he was yanked away from his design:
his daughter's kitten, too far up a tree,
had to be rescued. Undelightedly
he undertook to grapple with white pine,
up in whose jutting plumes of needles clung
that tiny fright incarnate and enfurred.
He got it down. His daughter's satisfaction
was ample, quick, and real. His forearm stung
with scratches, but his brain hummed with a word
found on a high branch, fathered by distraction.

Dec. 23

He's finished tacking up the Christmas garland
so it arrays the Parish Hall at one end,
loops of glistering tinsel off a rafter.
Nagged by Sunday School teachers, none of whom
could reach to do it, he brought up his ladder
and hammered through their bicker of suggestions
to pin the swags the way he damn well wanted.
Under this job tomorrow an eight-year-old
boy, a seven-year-old girl will cradle
a large, diapered baby doll between them,
while shepherds of the same age, some of them
notorious brats, stand burlap-clad with canes,
lording it over younger ones on all fours
and wrapped in artificial fleece, no lines
to learn, just lots of docile, brutish kneeling.
It's like this every year, the eve of the Eve;
hung up, the silvery furbelow now seems
to emphasize the bareness of the space
beneath it, wintry Bethlehem of worn
linoleum facing ranks of metal chairs
he set up once the ladies left him to it.
It will have to do. Only the garland
and the direction of the gathered chairs
will make this patch of floor into a stage.
Parents, onlookers will watch as children
pretend to be parents and onlookers
in a receding time, a distant place.
Tired, he folds his ladder, bumps it down

to stow it in the basement, takes a look
at the oil burner, hearing once again
that ticking noise he doesn't like. Upstairs,
although he never aimed to make a still life,
he's done just that in absentmindedness
on a west windowsill. But no one's here
(is it too early or is it too late?)
to watch the things glint when the white spear
of sunlight touches them: his laid-aside
claw hammer and a handful of long nails.
Instruments of the Passion. Tools of somebody's trade.

The Devil's Garden

Just how many geological sites
or isolated rocky oddities
has man, namer of place and thing, assigned
to the Antagonist? Not the least intending
to make an inventory, over the years
I've seen, to itemize only a few,
the jungly Florida sinkhole that they call
The Devil's Millhopper, the stony pit
the western Scots have dubbed The Devil's Washtub,
and near to here, on the next mountainside,
the globed "erratic boulder"—glacial litter—
locally known to be The Devil's Punchbowl.
None of them was especially terrifying.
Nor is this—but it can seem uncanny.
Halfway up the heavily wooded side
of this untaxing mountain, suddenly
growth ceases, yields to a broad tract
of barrenness, acres of rock no pine
or birch or aspen ever grapples onto;
whatever soil once was there was ferried
down out of sight in centuries of rains.
Naturally, no trees will mean no birds.
You find yourself humming to break the silence.
This is the landscape flayed, a gaunt substratum:
if not the bowels, the gallstones of the earth.
If the rocks weren't so smooth they might suggest
the rubble left from thunderous bombing raids,
but smooth they are, an unappealing gray,

ranging in size from cobbles down to scree.
And this is what they call The Devil's Garden.

Garden no sower's hand has blessed with seed,
ground that no root will get a purchase on,
heaped with the sad, unwholesome loaves that no
wheedling flattery will turn to bread . . .
one can appreciate the nomenclature.
The wilderness of western Massachusetts
can serve as well as any in the world
to show the sterile harvest of negation;
here is some land not good for anything
but to be daunted by, and that not often.
Left to itself, it never changes much.
Look now and remark with what fine guile,
deeding such hardluck parcels to the Devil,
we situate his foothold safely distant
from where we live and work and raise our own
plenteous crops, a skill passed down to us
by the first gardener (yes, remember), Cain.

Waiting Room

Here's where the unwell (sometimes chaperoned,
if they are fortunate, by the as yet
unsick) take seats to have their patience honed:
finding not much in last year's magazines,
or aqua tiles to count upon the floor,
or what remains of the mind's slender means
to purchase a few moments to forget
what they are waiting out or waiting for
beyond the inner door.

The Latest Sign

It's darn hard to keep up with euphemism.
Like an overnight flurry of powdered sugar,
it candies the landscape: lately, some well-meaning
soul in Town Hall, all sensitivity, gave
the residents a block down leave to change
their corner road sign to be less alarming.
It used to say, plainly enough, DEAD END.
Now, suddenly gentrified, it says
NO OUTLET. Is that really an improvement?
Maybe the old folks (pardon, senior citizens)
living there found the old sign too portentous.
It had a certain glamour, though, suggesting
Cagney-like gangsters gunned down in an alley.
NO OUTLET I find vastly more depressing—
summoning images of some regrettable
intestinal condition, or of endless
Sundays with in-laws, or a dingy, mirthless,
sub-Sartrean play transpiring in a basement
last-chance saloon (well, no, let's say café)
whose denizens discuss their angst and ours
for hours—three long interchangeable acts.
I'm glad it's not my street. It isn't even
called a street: its other sign calls it a "way."
(More wincing diction, tiptoeing around
a streak of asphalt married to the ground.)
It doesn't do to think too hard about

the signs that pin us down to our location.
They have too many undertones: it's best
to let your ear be deadened (sorry, numbed)
as soon as possible, as mine will be,
no doubt, by passing it day in, day out,
until it's just another sign to me.

The Arbor

Enter and find yourself enwrapped in green.
Ferns underfoot, vines walling in each side,
leaves coalescing in a roof provide
an ambience so nearly submarine
you wonder if you might have to grow gills
to stay in this domain of chlorophyll's.

After some moments, though, still breathing air
and thriving under that fine-woven shade
that lets in light only to stain it jade,
you see nestled in leaves what more is there:
grapes whose dimensions haven't yet surpassed
the size of peppercorns. They will at last,

and doff their camouflage, assuming tints
of Tyrian purple misting into ink.
Gladly to steep oneself, not just to think
but to watch thought grow ripe from greenest hints:
that is what vintage poets learned to do.
The marvel is, it might work here for you.

A Roadside Flock

The weather vane designer's rundown shop
can stay rundown: it's hardly even seen
by those who blink in passing or who stop
to blink again amid the bossy sheen

of roosters mobbing porch and forecourt, bright
as newly minted pennies, shimmering so
that one imagines each undimmed by night,
vain that no common dawn could make him crow.

Not only roosters—there's a whale or two,
a trotting horse. But fowl predominate,
and N and S and E and W
all come beneath their sway. Their high estate,

if crowning house or barn in fact is such,
may at first give them a heraldic thrill.
Before we yield to envy overmuch,
let's recollect what exaltation will

commit them to: their giddy doom to pivot,
prey to the winds that flounce about the sky.
It's not the life we'd live if we could live it.
And gleam gives way to verdigris, raised high

to weather drably, exiled from the ground . . .
Feel that? A hint of breeze. Birds of a feather,
their regal beaks shudder without a sound,
and all the copper flock turns tail together.

"Called Back"

—Inscription on Emily Dickinson's tombstone.

We came—a Century or so
Too late—to find you Home—
We paced your Father's House—We viewed
The Tokens that your Room

Exhibits—chief, the single Dress
Cased Head to Foot in Glass—
Demurely White and Cassock-like—
Its Buttons quaint to us—

Then went Outside—an easy Walk
To where your Kin conveyed
Your Quiet Form—whose Pilgrimage
Required their Parade—

Now we—who looked to find you Here—
Are once again reproved—
Your Granite Placard curtly hints
How far Away you've moved—

Gray Words hemmed by an Iron Fence—
Latticed—by mighty Trees—
Your Postscript to the World declares
How Potent Absence is

Up and Away

The brandished mirrors of the dew
grew restive as the daylight grew;
soon winked away, the myriad gleam
regrouped in subtle plumes of steam
that were as soon removed from sight—
all of this brief as it was bright.
We felt . . . I wouldn't say bereft,
but certainly abruptly left.
The world, indulging in its wont,
said, "Now you see it, now you don't."

The billion drops that dazzled there,
now lusterless and lost in air—
why such a rush to rarefy
and leave the meadow drab and dry?
Why couldn't they have stayed to fling
the morning sun at everything?
But if they hadn't turned to vapor,
would I be putting this on paper?
Worn out, perhaps, by shining so,
they found as comely a way to go,
and found in airy boundlessness
a fair exchange for shimmer. Yes,
one could do worse than evanesce.

Drowned Towns

for John Burt

I

Quabbin: in the tongue of the old people,
the Nipmuk tribe, the name means "many waters."
The sound of it is somehow waterlogged,
a muffled duck call in the fading light.
It is a confluence, dammed, diked, collected,
repository of rivercourse and rainfall.
Squinted at on the Massachusetts map
it looks like a schematic buzzard hunched
on a stubby branch. It came to roost there only
half a century back. For eons earlier
three veins of the Swift River, rich in trout,
bustled and brimmed through four small valley towns
to meet below them in a broader stream.

Those four towns had never a hope of growing
after they were bypassed by the railroad.
They didn't even have a hope of staying
once they attracted thirsty Boston's eye.
Dana, Enfield, Greenwich and Prescott lie
submerged beneath four hundred billion gallons.
Their destiny presents an object lesson
in the traditional civics of the Commonwealth:
to wit, what Boston wants, it gets.
(Or gets a part of: calculations vary
how many hundred thousands of piped gallons
leak out along the way there every year.)

II

This didn't take place overnight, of course.
For over a decade it was kicked around
the Legislature, challenged in the courts,
bruited in the press. Foresighted people
started to sell out, and the tax rolls shrank.
Nearing the end, the unwilling exodus
accelerated as the locust armies
of antique dealers and house salvagers
whiled away the weekends with their pillage.
Buildings went on the block: North Dana's school
was knocked down for $35. The Town Hall
in Enfield won the highest bid that day:
$350. (It was brick.)
Anything that wasn't bought or rustled
out of the place was bulldozed and then burned.
The inhabitants of thirty-four cemeteries
were scooped up and deported to a single
tastefully shrubbed, consolidated site,
tamped down, headstones planted in stiff new rows
with no attempt to keep the culled remains
together by town. (At this late date, new neighbors!)

Before this strenuous harvest of the dead,
before the purging of the ground by fire,
the late-to-leave performed their rituals
of severance: the Firemen's Farewell Ball
in Enfield, with its black-edged invitations,
where at the end the band played "Home, Sweet Home."
The last town meetings—see how the newspaper
posed this Selectman pointing an eraser

right at the spot—there!—on the schoolhouse globe
henceforth to be rubbed out of existence.
And the depleted, brave school graduations,
classes of children fewer than a dozen
delivering earnest speeches to their elders
on topics like "Our Debt to Civilization."
And singing: "Vesper Sparrows," "Faith of Our Fathers,"
and (for the recessional) "Auld Lang Syne."

Then the last decampments, the roads closing.
The valley scalped, burned over, deeply dredged.
The two great walls of earth and concrete mounting.

The reservoir took seven years to fill.

III

How many displaced townsfolk through the years
have stirred in sleep, revisiting the valley,
drawn back by the irresistible dream?
—You come to the center of town on your old bicycle
finding it all at first the way it was.
But there are no people walking the streets,
rocking on porches, looking out of windows.
On the picket fence of the house you're passing
the morning glory vines have been replaced
by tendrils of some rank, unlovely weed.
There is a silty, thwarted light on everything.
Look up: the sun's a muddled, wiggling yolk;
schools of fish go flickering in and out
of the Methodist Church belfry. Out of this depth

and hideous fluidity you wrench yourself,
gulping for air, and much relieved to breathe it.
Go there, though, on a summer afternoon.
The smooth, prosaic access road that ambles
into the corner set aside for parkland
leads to no tragic vision, just a view
of water up to its trick of aping sky—
blue vying with blue, above, below.
These tidy acres now are not the haunt
of human nightmare but of serene, dreamless
species who bring a touch of nature back
to soften all this mammoth engineering,
who drink but don't unduly foul the waters.
White-tailed deer, bobcat and wild turkey
browse in the fields and roam the posted woods.
Kept clean for fifty years, the sprawling lake
can be surveyed in all its magnitude
from a brutalist granite lookout tower
topping the highest hill. From there birdwatchers
swivel and tilt binoculars to catch
glimpses of eagles soaring in lordship over
waters no man fishes in by boat.
They have done well here—golden and bald eagles.
I have watched for it, but I have never seen
what Whitman saw one day: a pair in "dalliance":
"The rushing amorous contact high in space together,
The clinching interlocking claws, a living, fierce, gyrating
      wheel."
I have seen only solitary wheelings,
seemingly aimless till a taloned dive
ended everything for some fish or rodent.

IV

There is a small museum in New Salem,
up at the northern tip of the reservoir,
where you can see some remnants of what was.
Dismally cased in glass are antique buttons,
knitting needles, Grange medals, Indian arrowheads;
here's a militia drum, and someone's tuba,
a couple of woodstoves and, sitting nearby
like a surrealist pun, a stovepipe hat.
Other headgear: a Union soldier's cap,
the blue faded almost to the enemy's butternut.
There are three identical wedding dresses
worn by three nonidentical sisters.
You wonder at the sheer haphazardness
of things laid out and labeled to recall
the vanished towns—so sad a miscellany
it almost looks washed up by the rising waters.
Elderly docents, veterans of the deluge,
answer most questions vaguely, through a scrim
of chancy, rambling memory in which
some few things blink through sharply:
they all remember leaving for the last time.

It was a life; it may not have been much
of a living, judging from the ineffectual
examples here and there of local industries:
soapstone footwarmers, Shaker-style bonnets,
and the palmleaf fans and tablemats
that women wove as piecework in the home.
One of the few real factories specialized
in curiously segmented wooden boxes,

used to entrap and transport honeybees.
You can imagine the woeful hum you'd hear,
holding an occupied one up to your ear.
The clever, brass-hinged, combless hives
sit gaping now. The abducted swarms have flown.

V

Old citizens, solid
householders made
evictees by virtue
of eminent domain,
those of you who linger
skirting the watershed
furnish us a spectacle
that is pious, piteous,
or simply cautionary;
whether we attend
your faltering museum tours
or pace between the serried
tablets of your forebears'
second and, with some luck,
final resting place.
In the span of a few years
you incurred the lifetime's
buffetings, sunderings
that are the lot of all,
but meted out to most of us
over a longer siege:
the wiping from the map
of time-honored ways

to get from here to there,
the forced conversion
of matter testable by touch
to memory's errant mist.
You sit, a dwindling few,
across the road from this
man-made, middle-aged lake,
hallowing your relics
of the times before the flood.
Looking at them, at you,
how can we fail to feel
tremors of intimation?—
knowing that, behind our backs,
the water is always rising.

Snowplow in the Night

The Public Works Department juggernaut
mounted its customary grand onslaught
long after I, like most, had gone to bed.
Did it affect me? No one but the dead
could sleep through diesel-powered din like that.
Implacably compelling snow to scat,
cyclopean commotion cleared the road.
And that was my first hint that it had snowed.
Spirited out of clouds to drop or swirl,
then aggregate as ermine trimmed with pearl,
those bridal trappings that were just bulldozed
made their appearance while my eyes were closed.
Now that I look, what lingers to be seen
is worlds away from anything pristine.
The poet who lamented last year's snow
might have been stunned to see this midnight's go
from gossamer to gutter-hugging mound
nearly as quickly as it kissed the ground.
Men of the plow, I missed your surging by.
Here at the window, though, I wonder why
your gritty barrows lumped along the curb
have in their heaps such power to perturb.
Looking too long at sullied residue
that lines the road that leads to nowhere new,
I think of all the things I've slumbered through.

Espalier

Hugging its trellis, backed by sunny bricks,
this tree will never cast a shadow. Splayed
symmetrically, arboreal crucifix,
its aim in life appears to be to trade

its three dimensions for a tidier two.
You say it makes you wince, that rigid reach
to left and right. But all that gardeners do
along these lines ensures the tender peach

firm buttressing against the wind, and sun's
largesse enlarged on a south-facing wall.
Such fruits are juicier than unfettered ones
whose laden branches splinter as they sprawl.

What am I saying? What we call a fetter
may be a means of turning green to gold.
Words, I have found, abide the seasons better
spread to the light in meter's faithful hold.

Shoptalk: Ten Epigrams

Voices and Visions, Then and Now

Roused from his cozy bed among the swine,
Caedmon learned from an angel each bold line.
Would that such grace availed itself today
to Grunt, gone rooting for an M.F.A.

"Odi et Amo"?

She left. And still, he sat and wrote about
how he could not live with her nor without.
Hatred and love contended in his lyric.
Whichever won, the victory was Pyrrhic.

Last Ingredient

His lines were lacking zest.
Where, though, could he obtain
something he failed to feel?
No gusto there to peel
meant grating what you guessed:
that lemon of a brain.

Lowell's Legatees

A curious sacrament, this verse confession,
wherein the penitent proclaims aloud
the seamy details of each retrogression,
wheedling absolution from the crowd.

An Out-of-Print Avant-Garde Anthology

These poets who pursued *le dernier cri*
have found oblivion through cacophony.

Prosody Project

The kind of free verse I would find appealing
would steal from prose only those things worth stealing,
disdain the rest as journalistic dross.
Then loss of meter might not count as loss.

Lit. Crit.

Radiant words, what teases them to peel
your gleaming sheath apart to find the pith?
Ravaged, you let them dredge around by feel,
emptied of light they might have scanned it with.

A Thunderclap

Cloud-curtains, when they cracked,
paid heed to earthly laws:
the flashier the act,
the wilder the applause.

Reception after the Reading

After prolonged obeisance to Apollo
a nod to Dionysus ought to follow.

Plato Banishes the Poets

Word-benders, on your way!
Your songs can only mar
the mind with ecstasy,
jolting the state astray.
Transporting as you are,
transported you must be.

Waste

One of the geese, stereotypically silly,
has left an egg in plain sight at the edge
of the silty pond that only days ago
swallowed the last of its ice: the paper-white
shell against the new green of the grass tuft
she thought would do for a nest is almost
shouting for notice. Which it soon will get,
poised keen for calamity between
the bike path and the water's tarnished mirror.
Midnight snack for a skunk or a raccoon,
or handful for some unreflective child
to clamp and heave, it has already had
its future signed away by what appears
the unembarrassed absent-mindedness
of Nature. Nothing to do, it's cold already,
just as null as that antique darning egg
that used to pop up as an annual joke
in an Easter basket, unfunny even then.
Tantalized by its tactility,
I scan it one last time and do not touch.
Here where I see it I will see it gone
tomorrow, having done with its poor docile
journey back to the heedlessness it never
adequately escaped. If keeping track
of things were something I was better at,
I might adopt it as a white reminder,
something of worth abandoned that I ought
to pledge allegiance to even as I

in turn desert it, turning to walk on.
But could I fairly promise to remember?
Who am I to arraign the Great Carelessness,
given those hosts of tender true beginnings
molded in mind, each perfect as that oval
and pulsing with incipience, brought to light
only to pass through dormancy to doom,
finished by this brisk air I seem to thrive on?

A Paper Cut

Whatever first impressions may allege,
this poet's work does, after all, have edge—

witness my finger, slivered to the quick
as payback for its disapproving flick.

Granted, I turned the page with reckless haste,
calling no halt to justify my taste.

But does the stuff deserve a second reading?
Feel free to guess. It stings, but there's no bleeding.

Solving for X

Protean emblem, how to pin you down?
You are the unknown quantity in hiding
behind a blackboard's haze of wasted chalk,
mark on a treasure map a second look
proves innocent of place names or of bearings,
malefactor pursued through twenty chapters
to be unmasked by equally fictitious
detectives who would miss you in real life.
Miss you—because you flourish so profusely,
straddling so many contexts (sacred, sinister,
rarefied, common): sparkling in the dome's
mosaic, you are the monogram of Christ
or instrument of Andrew's martyrdom;
or, white on black, the femurs crossed beneath
buccaneer's merry bogy. Black on yellow
warns more mildly: railroad tracks ahead.
Sign of a kiss, and multiplying sign,
Caesar's 10, illiterate signature,
teacher's mark in the margin ("wrong again").
Antepenultimate character, you abut
a forking path that leads to the alphabet's
ultimate fizzle—snore in a comic strip—
while you, in suchlike sagas, replace the eyes
of two-dimensional victims just gunned down.
Unable to take form without a pause
and lifting of the pen, are you implying
that two strokes representing different meanings

cancel each other out, or one the other?
But one stroke leaves the other standing, starts
the latest round of tic-tac-toe. We live
webbed in the world's converging decussations,
no further away than our own shoelaces,
bemused by the plasticity of signs
that after some initial idle noticings
beckon our attention from all sides:
stitch of a little girl's sampler (1850),
weave in a wicker porch chair, fingers crossed
just now for luck; and here, facing the water,
sturdy tape bracing each staring window
in the gray lull before the hurricane hits.

Ant in Amber

Ever since Fate's undeviating thumb
englobed this ant in aromatic gum,
eons of weighty chafing in the earth
have milled it to a bauble of some worth.
Nature expended quite some enterprise
in getting this poor sap to fossilize.
Now honey-hued, translucent, it displays
intact the forager of former days:
every last leg the little soldier needed
is here embalmed, or we might say embeaded.
Didn't the Greeks believe such beads were spawned
as tears of sunset, hardened as next day dawned?
Knowing the source (a long-gone, weeping tree)
makes this a different kind of prodigy —
a model instance, maybe, of renewal —
interred as ant and disinterred as jewel.
Thus in our scale of values, though we can't
be sure it would appear so to the ant.

Wishing Well

Incredible to calculate how many
longings amass here. Each descending penny

carries a bid for love or luck, or sunny
weekends all summer, or (imagine!) money—

all on exhibit, that abounding range
of wants caressed by ripples. Just small change,

but, as we all by now must be aware,
it's not a good investment. Fair, unfair,

mosaicing the fountain floor, the votive
offerings wink at every shallow motive

that sent them to sit quiet, soak and grow:
our copper-scaled leviathan below.

Seed Catalogues in Winter

Daylilies for the ages, Four O'Clocks,
Bells of Ireland, Chinese Lanterns, tall
Siberian Iris, towering Hollyhocks,
dwarf Asters, Moonflowers, Morning Glories, all

blossom before us on the coffee table
in our mail-order plans for paradise.
Consulting these, Cain might have bested Abel
unbloodily. We leaf through sound advice

on climate zones and soil composition,
pH and compost, how much sun or shade
will nurse our seedlings on to their fruition.
Their destiny is plain: to be displayed,

a point that Breck's and Burpee's emphasize
with stunning color mugshots of their wares.
The perfect petals almost hypnotize—
so beautifully immune to weather scares,

invasive weeds, voracious pests, our own
perennially slipshod husbandry.
Ours is a yard where any seed that's sown
needs to wage war to reach maturity.

So much we know. But when the daily vista
is moody sky slung over wizened hedge

rooted in frozen mud, who could resist a
hankering to smooth down each ragged edge?

And yes, drifts of Delphiniums would be nice:
imagine, heaven-blue spires six months hence. . . .
As Samuel Johnson said of marrying twice,
how often hope outleaps experience.

A Flashback

I owe this to a twisted knee.
Limping upstairs reminded me
of early days when I would put
on the first step a cautious foot,
then draw the other up beside it.
Quicker, of course, each time I tried it,
but at its best my start-and-stop
was a slow way to reach the top.
When I got there and turned to see
the cliff I'd conquered manfully
dwindling toward a far-off floor,
I wasn't ready yet for more.
Taking the onus off my feet,
I went down tamely, on my seat.

Typo

As quick as words occur,
as quick as fingers drum,
something that yearns to err
taps out a sly outcome

I'd like not to erase.
See, by a single stroke,
wardrobe has given place
to *wordrobe*. Joycean joke,

wrong but so oddly right
a proofreader might think
pointless all oversight,
wit having seized the ink.

Jet sarong traipsing by—
might simple charm protect it?
Context demurs. I sigh,
bend forward and correct it.

Buyer's Remorse

Why did I buy that shirt
that mopes there in the closet
shaming its humbler neighbors?
Clearly, it isn't me:
its pinstripes yearn for a boardroom,
its finicky little tabs
that button behind a tie-knot
resist my struggling fingers
(aghast, perhaps, at my ties).
I've worn it only once,
and felt draped with imposture.
It's really meant for the cousin
who shows up overdressed
at the family Christmas dinner—
just part of the uniform
trumpeting his success.
On him it would look just right.
On me it seemed to be waiting
with fear and resignation
for the first gravy stain.
Bankerly stripes, drawn taut
against a glacial background:
what could be more correct
or more out of context, here?

But there's an odd thing lately.
We're getting used to each other,
as if so glaring a lack

of affinity makes a link.
There is another life
one might have had (or still might),
waiting to be tried on —
and isn't it worth something
to have this choice reminder,
this hint of it here in sight?

The Draft

Deputed to keep track
for midnight's census list,
intruding through some crack
that caulk or putty missed,

pencil of cold air,
what have you come to check?
I feel your tally there
on my unguarded neck.

Unwelcomely waylaying
one on his way to bed,
upending hair, conveying
some omen to be read,

ingressing breathily,
this grimly tapered gust
has got the drop on me.
Is it to say I must

regard myself a morsel
attractive to the Fates?
No, just one whose dorsal
flesh horripilates,

who can distinguish chill
per se from chill of fright,
at least for now. (There will
come a yet colder night.)

Letter of Recommendation

Miss A, who graduated six years back,
has air-expressed me an imposing stack
of forms in furtherance of her heart's desire:
a Ph.D. Not wishing to deny her,
I dredge around for something laudatory
to say that won't be simply a tall story;
in fact, I search for memories of her,
and draw a blank—or say, at best a blur.
Was hers the class in that ungodly room
whose creaking door slammed with a sonic boom,
whose radiators twangled for the first
ten minutes, and then hissed, and (this was worst)
subsided with a long, regretful sigh?
Yes, there, as every Wednesday we would try
to overlook cacophony and bring
our wits to bear on some distinguished thing
some poet sometime wrote, Miss A would sit
calm in a middle row and ponder it.
Blonde, I believe, and quiet (so many are).
A dutiful note-taker. Not a star.
Roundheads and Cavaliers received their due
notice from her before the term was through.
She wrote a paper on . . . could it have been
"Milton's Idea of Original Sin"?
Or was it "Deathbed Imagery in Donne"?
Whichever, it was likely not much fun
for her. It wasn't bad, though I've seen better.
But I can hardly say that in a letter

like this one, now refusing to take shape
even as wispy memories escape
the reach of certitude. Try as I may,
I cannot render palpable Miss A,
who, with five hundred classmates, left few traces
when she decamped. Those mortarboard-crowned faces,
multitudes, beaming, ardent to improve
a world advancing dumbly in its groove,
crossing the stage that day—to be consigned
to a cold-storage portion of the mind . . .
What could be sadder? (She remembered *me*.)
The transcript says I gave Miss A a B.

Out of Character

The colleague almost no one else could stand—
(at meetings he would lecture the Department
on what they ought to know, i.e., what art meant),
a pest who never did a thing unplanned

or unnarrated, pompous to his peers,
inflicting monologue on the unwary
who hadn't yet learned his itinerary,
anesthetizing classes down the years,

brandishing that unfinished manuscript
decades of secretaries came to dread—
unnerved them all one day by dropping dead.
Once they allowed themselves some less tight-lipped

reactions, they agreed: the place would now
be far more livable. No more harangues,
even the tenderest sighed, and felt no pangs
till their next meeting, when they noticed how

lack of those canned digressions, even lack
of that annoying punctuating cough
threw their own pace of conversation off,
summoning their bemused attention back

to note his present absence at the table.
Could irritation be like joy or love,
something we miss, and need some quota of
to live as vividly as we are able?

Making Do

Who can forget the ripple of disgust
that twisted the piano tuner's lip
on viewing the repair some former owner
(oh no, not us) had made with a bootlace?
It did the job, holding the pedal up.
But who could fault his scandalized recoil?
By now we ought to be familiar with
that look of flouted, outraged expertise
surveying the offence of ignorant
contrivances, cheap shortcuts, slovenly
expedients only a manic devotee
of puttering could approve or even think of.
Just so, when we moved in, the electrician
stared at the spiderweb of circuitry
some tinkering precursor hooked on wiring
trellised the basement with. And the house painter
almost swallowed his cigarette when he saw
the alligatoring my hapless, hand-done
sanding had left sitting on the clapboards.

Inured to such embarrassments, I grant
their right to be disgruntled: well-equipped
professionals are honor bound to scorn
the botch and haste of clueless amateurs.
(Although, come to think of it, a major
part of their living comes from cleaning up
our mean shifts or mad ambitious messes.)
I envy their straight saw-cuts, their rock-steady
hands with a ruler, fully furnished toolkits,

top grade hardware, knowing just how poorly
versed and outfitted most are doomed to be.
When shall I ever use the right length nail,
or hang a picture not a smidge too high?
Don't we, most of us, mince up an onion
to take the place of seldom-bought shallots?
Children sent to school wearing knee patches
that almost matched, but didn't quite, have trudged
into adulthood, peering at the world
through glasses mended at the nose with tape.
Dumbly or spiritedly we improvise,
make do with what we have in the brief time
allotted to these tasks that from above
must look like kindergarten projects done
with sometimes careful, often clumsy fingers.
Making do, we don't always do badly.
I think of Dr. Johnson's blind housekeeper
judging the level of the tea she poured
by holding a practiced finger in the cup;
or of my Revolutionary ancestor,
doing his bit by firing his cannon
into the red lines till his powder patch
burned through, after which he used both thumbs
and several fingers. It was what he had.

Static

A cold, keen-edged day.
When she pulled her sweater off
over her hair, her

hair yearned after it,
giving off a crackle like
half-smothered fireworks.

He watched it slowly
settling to her shoulders in
wisps of spent charges;

air all around seemed
vested with energies it
couldn't well contain.

When he brushed past her
a twinge, an electrified
touché, unseen but

felt by both of them,
shot prickling from her hand
to his (or might it

have been vice versa?
He'd been scuffing the rug, as
usual, and as

usual, she wished
he'd learn to pick up his feet).
Neither of them said

a word, but each smiled
to see another smile sparked,
the circuit working.

Pilgrims

White as a baby's tooth, the little church
pokes up from the apostate wilderness
of onetime farms gone back to scrubby woods.
Everything's cradled snug in sabbath peace
as we approach, but suddenly, as if
we'd tripped a wire, there is a soft moan
and wheeze set off inside—the balky organ—
and then the singing, adamant and loud,
vehement exhalations taking heart
from heaving all together, as though one
ultimate heave could raise the clapboard box
off its foundation, scooting it to heaven
on a self-generated gust of rapture.
Choir practice, probably, this being
Saturday afternoon. Pent in their resonant
unornamented boards, the choir must
comprise a great part of the congregation,
so dollhouse-like the building is. The hymn
trumpets a challenge to the tuckered-out
surrounding countryside to the effect of
Hear and be saved—which is, of course, beyond
its compass, sunk in drought-depleted stupor.
Casual, sweating passersby like us
may not intend to pay much greater heed;
but a few words do pelt us, slipping through
the chuffed accompaniment, the weighty drone.
Something about "O Savior, when we die

(de-dum, de-dum) thy dwelling place on high."
Words are prone to blur in the fervent yearning
broadcast from the louvered bottom panes
of those embattled-looking pointy windows.
Haunting the air, it cannot stir the dust
even as much as we do, shuffling past.
While we're still in earshot, the sound dies.
Rehearsal must be over. Yes, they're coming
out now, and I count them, half a dozen
women and four men. They clamber into
a decommissioned school bus, painted blue,
which we now see was parked around in back.
And we, wrapped in heat and resumed silence,
what are we out here looking for today?
We keep on going, down to the dry creek
to hunt for arrowheads. It's said to be
the place for this, but after a hot hour
of scrabbling through the pebble beds we find
exactly two, a flint for each of us.
Chipped to a razor-edge, they're tapered to
carpenter-gothic points much like the windows
out of which poured the ministry of song.
Which are the points that nick the soul more keenly—
those of the lost or those of the lingering tribe?

September Brownout

Dry summer means a fall
drabber than fall should be.
Once green has withered, all
dismayed leaf-peepers see

is one great wave of rust
corroding hill and dale.
Impotent to combust,
the scenery's gone stale;

and we, bereft of color,
discover that our own
demeanor has grown duller,
assumed a sepia tone.

Resigned to being scanted
of gold and crimson days,
we'll take no more for granted
the maple's yearly blaze,

nor doubt the arid power
and paradox of drought,
that with each missing shower
ensures a fire put out.

Other Eyes

Potato's

This tuber's dark protuberance aches to be
above ground, where there's so much more to see,

but lacking claws to scrabble like a mole
its tunnel upward to an exit hole,

it gambles all on its remaining hope—
the sprout it nudges up, the periscope.

Peacock's

The evil eye, enshrined and multiplied,
fanned out and flaunted in the strut of pride?

Fatuous folklore. Such eyes by the tailful
worship the sun, exuding nothing baleful,

offering tribute with their iridescence.
Only on us has pride bestowed its essence.

Hurricane's

Everything has a center. This is yours:
here, after all those savage slamming doors,

your inner sanctum of dumbfounding quiet,
turning a blind eye to winds at riot.

Seeing's believing. Glimpsing void, we guess
that mayhem is a mask for emptiness.

Daisy

Not often now in flower or in word
is *day's eye* even dimly seen or heard.

Our Anglo-Saxon's rusty. But the gaze
that suddenly meets ours on summer days

can still remind us: little drop of sun
staring from petals, metaphor not done.

Remainders

This two-foot stack of last year's ballyhooed
up-to-the-minute masterpiece gives pause.
Scanning the blurbs by now feels almost rude.
So much for all that critical applause

boosting these bouts of passion no one bought.
Imagine all the hours of sweating ink,
flailing in chapters feverishly wrought.
Slashed to three-ninety-eight. It makes you think,

and gives the author's photo a stunned look,
as though he'd glimpsed the tail end of his story.
No matter how much agony it took,
unless it's read it's only inventory.

QWERTY

The quick red fox our fingers trained to jump
over the lazy brown dogs so that we
could tell our keys were working properly
has come to a full stop. His russet rump,

that levitated on so many pages,
can loll at ease, ringed by his treasured tail.
Now on his own, he leaves no paper trail,
and though his years of service brought no wages

our kind neglect should let him rest unseen
and unmolested, thanks to this refinement—
no need to test these pixels for alignment.
Could he be lurking, though, behind the screen,

unready for a life unmonitored,
yellow eyes puzzled, wanting to know why
we'd let him, like those logy canines, lie?
Hunters of words, we roused him with a word;

quick on the jump but not quick to forget,
his ears are pricked for the old click-and-clack
that called him periodically back
to scramble madly through the alphabet.

Now and Then

"Now then," I said, and noticed again how
the now my tongue had sounded was no more;
it was now then, or then a newer now.
Mere sanity demands that we ignore

the awful ease of now becoming then,
flexing backward or forward from its point.
But be it understood: no matter when,
the time we spend or waste is out of joint.

Well, I'm still here, and it's a problem.
I didn't realize it till hours after
I'd watched all the millennial folderol
on TV in the lounge with all the residents
who aren't fussed into going to bed early—
a lot of fireworks trying to light up
one midnight like a dark tide washing round
the globe, engulfing each meridian.
(And all this a year early, but persuading
people of that was always a lost cause—
teaching school for more than thirty years
taught me how little people like to count.)
Anyway, I was in bed, drifting off,
when suddenly it flashed before my eyes:
the tombstone that I ordered for my husband
right after he died some years ago.
Simple inscription: his name and his dates,
and, since I assumed I would end up
in the same place, my own name following,
my birthdate, and (as I now saw, aghast)
19 with a blank two digits wide.
What a way to get tripped up by the calendar!
It seemed to make sense at the time, but now
the vision of the innocent, mistaken
oblong of pink granite seemed to blush
more than it does even in noonday glare.
I chose the pink because it somehow seemed

a little more alive than gray or white.
It holds its own, surrounded by the snow
or springtime's green or summer's wilted grass.
I always liked it. I just wasn't thinking.
19 blank! Blank was how I felt,
then furious. How could I have signed for that,
and how, at this late date, could it be fixed?
Chip out 19 and have it look a mess,
or have both dates removed as if to say
my ultimate age is nobody's damned business?
Could I perhaps plant some straggly shrub
and train it artfully to mask the dates?
Or should it just be left, no worse a lie
than many you can read in cemeteries:
"Dearly Beloved" must at least sometimes
be something of a stretch. It was absurd,
sitting there in the dark of New Year's Day
of Y2K with hours to go till dawn
worrying over such a thing. I wondered
what Herman, resting there below his own
unimpeachable dates, would make of it.
Often enough I wonder what he'd think
of all the things he didn't live to see
but hardly could be pitied much for missing:
gangsta rap, Jolt Cola, SUVs,
inline skating, online trading, out-of-line
politicians, MTV, or even,
come to think of it, the recent me,
still here, thanks to what we've learned to call
Assisted Living. He would probably
just laugh, and maybe that's what I should do,

over this mishap—small compared with plenty
of worries no doubt keeping from their sleep
people the world over, sick of fireworks,
knowing themselves now doomed to live past 20.

A Drained Fountain

This nameless naiad hasn't got a prayer
of filling the wide bowl her stepping stool
stands in the middle of, a granite stilt.
Blind to the disappearance of her pool,
holding an urn still at a lavish tilt,
she perseveres, pouring air into air.

A bird, inquisitive, who wet his wings
daily in ripples brimming at her feet,
lights on her earnest, weatherbeaten head
but soon departs to find a cheerier seat.
The backdrop trees will jettison their dead
to line this basin once alive with springs

sooner than not—the nights are that much colder.
Nothing can faze this maiden, though. Her poise,
braving the halt imposed on her cascade,
can almost conjure back its pattering noise,
its rainbow glints. She labors undismayed,
and if it's labor lost, nobody's told her.

Amnesia: Fragments

It's nothing like the movies. Absent data
never come drifting back as clouds of mist
disperse to the accompaniment of trills
fluttering off the high strings of a harp.
Always more sudden: like the wary deer
riveted to the roadside by your headlights,
or the meteor streak you merely happen
to ambush, glancing up at the night sky.

Faces come back without their names, or names
without their faces. My own face this morning,
recognizable as myself, whoever
that might be, yet nothing nameable.
Just a man shaving—one skill he's retained.

Here, yes, there's mist: mist on the mirror.

What about objects, scenes, the déjà-vu
induced by an old-fashioned water cooler
with conical paper cups, each one a tiny
dunce cap, haunting a shadowed office alcove?

Or the faint clash of a woman's bracelets,
the votive glow of a restaurant table candle
against her cheek? When and in what city,
fair or forlorn, were these part of my life?

Names without faces, curious or comical,
suddenly there, as if swept in by a wave.
Boomer was one. Flitcraft was another.
Could I be either? I was found without papers.

Also the dates, equally unaccountable.
Why am I seized by 1968?
Somehow it brings to mind a smell of burning.
I have the feeling nothing has been the same
since then. How old am I? Was I political,
the way most people were who nowadays
find different things to occupy their minds?

Identifying marks identify only
when the right memory's mirror throws them back.
Mine sit dead on the skin, evoking no
answering image. Well, do I want to know
where the burn scar on my left wrist came from?

If ever it all came back, splendid or terrible,
this is how it would feel: the way it felt
when I was a child (somewhere) visiting
(someone's) farm. My first time in the hen house,
I reached into a nest and felt the eggs
in all their fragile, treasurable intactness,
and lifting one up wanted to hold it always.